INDIANS OF EASTERN NORTH AMERICA

WORLD BOOK

World Book
a Scott Fetzer company
Chicago
www.worldbookonline.com

World Book, Inc.
233 N. Michigan Avenue
Chicago, IL 60601
U.S.A.

For information about other World Book publications, visit our
Web site at **http://www.worldbookonline.com** or call
1-800-WORLDBK (967-5325).
For information about sales to schools and libraries, call
1-800-975-3250 (United States), or **1-800-837-5365 (Canada)**.

Library of Congress Cataloging-in-Publication Data

Indians of Eastern North America.
    p. cm. -- (Early peoples)
  Includes index.
  Summary: "A discussion of the Indians of the eastern part of
North America, including who the people were, where they lived,
the rise of civilization, social structure, religion, art and architecture,
science and technology, daily life, entertainment and sports, and
fall of civilization. Features include timelines, fact boxes, glossary,
list of recommended readings and web sites, and index"--Provided
by publisher.
  ISBN 978-0-7166-2138-6
  1. Indians of North America--Canada, Eastern--Juvenile literature.
  2. Indians of North America--East (U.S.)--Juvenile literature.
  I. World Book, Inc.
  E78.E2I53 2009
  974.004'97--dc22

                    2008040796

Printed in China by Leo Paper Products Ltd.,
Heshan, Guangdong
2nd printing June 2010

STAFF

EXECUTIVE COMMITTEE
President
  Paul A. Gazzolo
Vice President and Chief Marketing Officer
  Patricia Ginnis
Vice President and Chief Financial Officer
  Donald D. Keller
Vice President and Editor in Chief
  Paul A. Kobasa
Director, Human Resources
  Bev Ecker
Chief Technology Officer
  Tim Hardy
Managing Director, International
  Benjamin Hinton

EDITORIAL
Editor in Chief
  Paul A. Kobasa
Associate Director, Supplementary
Publications
  Scott Thomas
Managing Editor, Supplementary
Publications
  Barbara A. Mayes
Senior Editor, Supplementary Publications
  Kristina Vaicikonis
Manager, Research, Supplementary
Publications
  Cheryl Graham
Manager, Contracts & Compliance
  (Rights & Permissions)
  Loranne K. Shields

Administrative Assistant
  Ethel Matthews
Editors
  Nicholas Kilzer
  Scott Richardson
  Christine Sullivan

GRAPHICS AND DESIGN
Associate Director
  Sandra M. Dyrlund
Manager
  Tom Evans
Coordinator, Design Development and
Production
  Brenda B. Tropinski

EDITORIAL ADMINISTRATION
Director, Systems and Projects
  Tony Tills
Senior Manager, Publishing Operations
  Timothy Falk

PRODUCTION
Director, Manufacturing and Pre-Press
  Carma Fazio
Manufacturing Manager
  Steve Hueppchen
Production/Technology Manager
  Anne Fritzinger
Production Specialist
  Curley Hunter
Proofreader
  Emilie Schrage

MARKETING
Chief Marketing Officer
  Patricia Ginnis
Associate Director, School and Library
Marketing
  Jennifer Parello

Produced for World Book by
  White-Thomson Publishing Ltd.
  +44 (0) 845 362 8240
  www.wtpub.co.uk
  Steve White-Thomson, President

Writer: Barbara Davis
Editor: Steven Maddocks
Designer: Simon Borrough
Photo Researcher: Amy Sparks
Map Artist: Stefan Chabluk
Illustrator: Adam Hook (p. 37)
Fact Checker: Chelsey Hankins
Proofreader: Catherine Gardner
Indexer: Nila Glikin

Consultant:
Amy C. Schutt
Department of History
State University of New York College
at Cortland

TABLE OF CONTENTS

Glossary There is a glossary on pages 60-61. Terms defined in the glossary are in type **that looks like this** on their first appearance on any spread (two facing pages).

Additional Resources Books for further reading and recommended Web sites are listed on page 62. Because of the nature of the Internet, some Web site addresses may have changed since publication. The publisher has no responsibility for any such changes or for the content of cited sources.

WHO WERE THE INDIANS OF EASTERN NORTH AMERICA?

American Indians have lived in the eastern part of North America for at least 12,000 years. Those who first inhabited this area left no record. However, **archaeologists** *(AHR kee OL uh jihstz)* have gained insights into how they lived by studying what they did leave behind. Human and animal bones, tools, pottery, carved figures, and other items offer a picture, however hazy, of eastern North America's first peoples.

The Indians who lived in what is now southeastern Canada and the eastern United States are usually divided into two **culture** groups: the Northeast culture group and the Southeast culture group. The territory of the two cultures covers a vast area. It extends from the Atlantic coast in the east to the Mississippi River in the west and from the Great Lakes in the north to the coast of the Gulf of Mexico in the south. Northeast and Southeast Indians, even those who lived thousands of miles apart, shared certain characteristics. These characteristics developed as a result of living in the great North American forests.

Pattern of Life

At the end of the last **ice age,** the Eastern Indians were **nomadic** hunters. They lived in small family groups and followed the herds of **mastodons** *(MAS tuh donz)* and woolly mammoths. As the climate warmed, these giant **mammals,** which had depended on ice age conditions for survival, became **extinct.** The Indians adapted to the changes in their environment by becoming **hunter-gatherers.** They hunted such game as elk, deer, and bear, and they fished in rivers and lakes. They also gathered edible plants.

Later, groups began planting crops, including corn, beans, and squash. Hunter-gatherer families no longer needed to be constantly on the move in search of food. They began to settle in villages. In some of the southern territories, the villages grew into large towns. Groups that shared a language and customs began to form into **tribes.**

▲ Archaeologists in Pennsylvania sift soil in search of Seneca and Iroquois **artifacts.**

Northeast Indians

In the Northeast, the Mohawk *(MOH hawk)*, Oneida *(oh NY duh)*, Onondaga *(ON uhn DAW guh)*, Seneca *(SEHN uh kuh)*, Cayuga *(kay YOO guh)*, and Huron *(HYUR uhn)* tribes spoke languages that belong to the Iroquoian *(IHR uh KWOY uhn)* language family. The Abenaki *(ah buh NAH kee)*, Wampanoag *(WAHM puh NOH ag)*, Narragansett *(NAR uh GAN siht)*, Pequot *(PEE kwot)*, Powhatan *(POW uh TAN)*, and Massachusett *(MAS uh CHOO siht)* spoke Algonquian *(al GONG kee uhn)* languages. Iroquoian and Algonquian peoples later independently formed powerful **confederacies**, or leagues. These leagues bound neighboring tribes together under one government.

Southeast Indians

The tribes of the Southeast cultural area included the Cherokee *(CHEHR uh kee)*, Chickasaw *(CHIHK uh saw)*, Creek, Natchez *(NACH ihz)*, and Seminole *(SEHM uh nohl)*. The Natchez were noted for their cities in which many thousands of people lived. They developed a highly structured society in which people were organized into ranks. The king held the highest rank, and the farmer the lowest. As in the Northeast, some of the peoples of the Southeast formed confederacies for the benefit of all member tribes.

▶ Indians used the distinctive white bark of birches, which grew in abundance in northeastern and parts of southeastern North America, for canoes, containers, clothing, and shelter. The Indians of eastern North America were highly dependent on trees to provide a wide range of essential goods.

RED PAINT PEOPLE

Archaeologists have discovered ancient burial pits dating from around 6,000 years ago in Newfoundland in eastern Canada. The pits contained tools, carved figures of animals, and other goods carefully arranged alongside the buried dead. In addition, everything in the pits was covered with a reddish powder. Investigations revealed that the powder was ground-up hematite *(HEHM uh tyt)*, a mineral common to the area. After the discovery of similar sites nearby, **anthropologists** *(AN thruh POL uh jihstz)* called the Indian culture who lived in the area the Red Paint People.

A Land of Trees and Water

The Eastern Indians' homeland included millions of square miles of forest and thousands of lakes and rivers. These habitats supported a wide variety of animals and plants. The Indians exploited these natural resources for food, clothing, and shelter.

The Northeastern Environment

The **tribes** of the Northeast lived in an area that covered part of present-day eastern Canada, the New England and Great Lakes states, and parts of Virginia and North Carolina. In this area, the winters are cold, and the summers are warm. There is enough rainfall to support lush forests of elm, maple, chestnut, hickory, birch, oak, and pine. The Indians used wood and bark from these trees to make a range of essential goods, from shelters and means of transportation to clothing and cooking pots. The forests provided not only wood but also a habitat for various game animals that provided the Indians with food.

Most Northeast tribes lived close to rivers, streams, or lakes, where they fished and harvested freshwater plants for food. For those tribes that lived along the Atlantic coast, saltwater fish, crustaceans (*kruhs TAY shuhnz*), and **mollusks** (*MOL uhskz*) were important sources of food.

The Southeastern Environment

The Indians of the Southeast lived in an area that stretched from the Atlantic Ocean in the east to present-day Texas in the west. The northern portion of their territory covered parts of present-day Virginia, West

▼ The Northeast Indian cultural area extended from southeastern and south-central Canada to the southern Appalachian Mountains and the Ohio River Valley. It stretched from the Atlantic coast in the east to the Mississippi River Valley in the West.

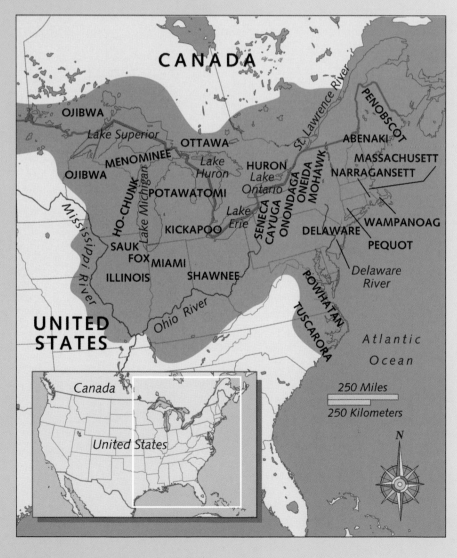

Virginia, North Carolina, South Carolina, Tennessee, and Kentucky, and small areas in Missouri and Arkansas. The southern portion encompassed present-day Georgia, Alabama, Mississippi, and Louisiana and parts of Arkansas, Oklahoma, and eastern Texas.

The Southeast forests were mainly yellow pine, but hemlock, oak, cypress, tulip poplar, and gum were also common in certain areas. In addition to woodlands, the Southeast had extensive marshland and in southern Florida, subtropical plant life. Thanks to ample rainfall, a warm climate, and rich soil, the Southeast Indians were able to grow much of their own food. The region's numerous waterways, saltwater and freshwater, were also rich sources of plant and animal life.

The abundance of local resources allowed many of the Southeast tribes to remain in one place for long periods of time rather than live a **nomadic** lifestyle. As a result, some of the largest and most complex of all Indian settlements were found in this cultural area.

◀ The Southeast Indian cultural area extended from the southern Appalachian Mountains to present-day Florida and the Gulf of Mexico. It stretched from the Atlantic Coast to the Mississippi River and beyond into present-day Louisiana, Arkansas, and Texas.

WOODLAND DEER

Deer were among the most important animals to Eastern Indian tribes. Indians ate deer meat for food and used deer hides for clothing. They carved arrowheads from antlers. Even deer hooves were useful; the Indians boiled them to make glue.

Notable Achievements

The complex government system developed by the Iroquois *(IHR uh kwoy)*, a group of northeastern **tribes**, was one of the most impressive achievements of the Indians of the East Coast. Sometime after A.D. 1450, the Seneca, Cayuga, Onondaga, Oneida, and Mohawk tribes formed a league known as the Iroquois Confederacy.

A council of 50 chiefs, or **sachems** *(SAY chuhmz)*, governed the Iroquois **Confederacy.** The elder women from each **clan** within the five tribes selected these chiefs. They chose a chief on the basis of his leadership qualities and past accomplishments. The elder women could also remove a chief who put his own interests ahead of those of his tribe or of the League. All of the clans were represented on the council.

The Great Binding Law

The League developed a complex **constitution** called the Great Binding Law. This law defined how the League was structured and how it would operate. The law gave every tribe, regardless of its size, a voice in the League's affairs.

The Great Binding Law governed many aspects of Iroquois life. It set down where and how to hold councils and how to trade with other Indians. The law even specifically stated that chestnut wood should not be used for the Council Fire. Some **anthropologists** believe that chestnut wood may have been banned because burning chestnut wood pops noisily and throws off sparks. The chiefs probably did not want the fire to create a distraction.

▶ The Iroquois lived in **longhouses,** which had an entrance at each end and separate sections within. The tribes of the Iroquois confederacy thought of their territory as a vast longhouse in which each tribe occupied a particular section. The Onondaga lived in the center of the confederacy's lands and were viewed as the keepers of the council fire. (In a longhouse, the main fire was at the center). The Mohawk's territory was the farthest east. They were seen as the keepers of the confederacy's eastern door. The Seneca were the keepers of the western door.

▲ *Sequoyah*, an 1830 portrait by Henry Inman after Charles Bird King. Sequoyah is credited with inventing the Cherokee writing system, the only writing ever developed by North American Indians.

The Great Binding Law bound the tribes of the Iroquois Confederacy into a single nation. By the mid-1660's the confederacy ruled around 10,000 people and was the largest and most powerful Indian **alliance** in North America.

The Cherokee Writing System

In the early 1800's, a Cherokee named Sequoyah *(sih KWOY uh)* developed a set of symbols, each of which represented a syllable in the Cherokee language. This system came to be called Sequoyah's **Syllabary** *(SIHL uh BEHR ee)*, which the Cherokee leaders accepted in 1821. Within a short time, thousands of Cherokee had learned to read and write their language. In 1828, the Cherokee National Council published America's first Indian newspaper. Sequoyah's Syllabary was the only writing ever developed by North American Indians.

MOUND BUILDERS

▼ Miamisburg Mound in southwestern Ohio was built by the Adena. It sits on a bluff about 100 feet (30 meters) high. The mound itself has a circumference of 877 feet (267 meters). When it was completed sometime between 800 B.C. and A.D. 100, it was more than 70 feet (21 meters) high.

DICKSON MOUNDS

One way archaeologists can learn about ancient peoples is by digging up their graves. However, many cultures, including many modern American Indians, see this practice as disrespectful and oppose the display of their ancestors' skeletons and holy objects in museums. In 1927, Don Dickson began excavating ancient Indian burial mounds on his family's property above the Illinois River near Havana, Illinois. He removed only the dirt from around the skeletons, leaving in place the bones and artifacts. Dickson later built a museum over the open mound, which allowed visitors to view the remains of the ancient peoples. Concerns of American Indians led the state of Illinois in 1992 to close to the public the actual burial site while maintaining a museum devoted to the people buried there.

Archaeologists have learned a great deal about some of the Indians who lived in eastern North America by excavating their earthen mounds. These unusual structures had a variety of purposes.

The Adena Culture

People of the Adena *(uh DEE nuh)* **culture** built some of the earliest mounds. The Adena lived from about 600 to 100 B.C. in the Ohio River valley and in present-day West Virginia, Kentucky, and Indiana. They built small mounds of earth over burial pits. The process was lengthy; the mound builders carried container after container of dirt and piled it over the pit.

Some graves contained **artifacts**. These items included carved **pendants** made of stone and

copper, stone smoking pipes, pearl beads, and engraved **mica** tablets. The graves with artifacts seem to have contained people of high rank in Adena society. Other, simpler graves contained only a few goods or none at all.

The Hopewell Tradition

Anthropologists believe that the Hopewell culture grew out of the Adena culture. The Hopewell culture lasted from around 100 B.C. to A.D. 500 and covered a much larger territory than the Adena. Archaeologists have found Hopewell artifacts throughout most of the midwestern and eastern United States.

The Hopewell mounds are generally much larger than those built by the Adena. Some are as high as 30 to 40 feet (9 to 12 meters). One of the largest Hopewell sites, found in Newark, Ohio, covered an area measuring 4 square miles (10.4 square kilometers). It contained the remains of hundreds of people who had been buried at different times.

Not only were the Hopewell sites larger than those of the Adena, the **grave goods** found there were more varied and of higher craftsmanship. The variety of grave goods suggests that the Hopewell developed a vast trading network. Graves in Ohio and at other Hopewell sites contained headdresses made from Great Lakes copper; spearheads and knives made of **obsidian** found in the Black Hills of South Dakota; and drinking cups made from **conch** *(konch)* shells from the Atlantic Ocean or the Gulf of Mexico. Beautifully crafted animal and human figurines are evidence of the skill of the Hopewell artisans.

◀ A carved wooden Hopewell figurine dating from between 300 B.C. and A.D. 500. Anthropologists believe the knot over the figure's forehead may represent a single horn, a symbol that the Hopewell used to identify a **medicine man.**

THE MISSISSIPPIANS

Beginning around A.D. 900, an important **culture** developed in the Mississippi Valley in parts of what are now Illinois, Missouri, and Tennessee. Like the Adena and Hopewell Indians, the Mississippians (MIHS *uh SIHP ee uhnz*) were mound builders.

Shared Traditions

Mississippian Indians shared some traditions with the earlier Hopewell culture. Both groups had a well-organized society and wide trade networks. Indians of both cultures farmed as well as hunted. They created everyday objects of great beauty. The main difference between the groups is one of scale: Mississippians expanded on Hopewell traditions by constructing huge mounds. These mounds became the focus for large towns.

Ancient Cities

Mississippian Indians' communities featured homes built around central plazas where residents bought and sold food and other goods. These homes were built on mound terraces. Mississippian society had a rigid structure.

MISSISSIPPIAN RITUAL AND ART

Mississippian craftsmen made some unique, but grim objects. Their pottery, jewelry, and masks feature images of human sacrifice. Much of their art includes images of skulls, bones, and weeping eyes. Archaeologists have found these objects throughout the region inhabited by the Mississippians. These findings suggest that all peoples of the Mississippian culture shared similar social structure, religious beliefs, and methods of warfare.

▼ The Cahokia Mounds State Historic Site in Collinsville, Illinois, is the location of what is believed to have once been the largest city of the Mississippian culture, with 8,000 to 40,000 inhabitants at its peak. There are several mounds of different sizes within this area. Monk's Mound (below) is the largest human-made earthen mound in North America: about 100 feet (30 meters) high, 955 feet (291 meters) long, and 775 feet (236 meters) wide. Archaeologists have found evidence that a large structure—perhaps a temple or the residence of a chief—once stood atop the mound.

A Mississippian pottery vase, from about A.D. 1000, depicts a human being. Archaeologists believe the figure's weeping eyes suggest that the Mississippians drew a symbolic connection between tears and rain.

A house's position on the terrace indicated its owner's social rank: the higher the house, the more important its owner. The king and his relatives had palaces on top of the highest mounds. Temples were also built on the highest mounds. Below them on smaller mounds were the houses of priests and **nobles**. Common people lived in huts that surrounded the mounds.

The largest Mississippian settlement, Cahokia *(kuh HOH kee uh)*, was located near the Mississippi River in present-day Illinois. The site features more than 100 earthen mounds covering an area of about 6 square miles (16 square kilometers). **Archaeologists** believe that 10,000 to 20,000 people may have lived at Cahokia at its peak (A.D. 1050–1150). Monk's Mound at Cahokia is the largest earthwork mound in the Americas. The four-level mound is about 100 feet (30 meters) high and was once topped by a structure that rose an additional 48 feet (14.6 meters). Archaeologists believe that this was probably the residence of Cahokia's king.

Mississippians and Mesoamericans

The Mississippian temple mounds in some ways resemble the temple pyramids that were built in ancient Mexico and other parts of **Mesoamerica**. Yet there are differences. The Mesoamericans built their pyramids entirely from stone. The Mississippians built their mounds from dirt and used wooden logs for the stairways.

Nevertheless, the similarities suggest that the Mississippian Indians had contact with peoples far to the south. The groups may have come into contact while traveling along trading routes. Mississippian burial sites contained objects with images of human sacrifice and representations of human skulls. Such items were features of Mesoamerican culture, which experts believe the Mississippian Indians adopted.

Influence on the Southeast

The Mississippian culture spread throughout much of the Southeast cultural area, and its influence can be traced in many Southeast **tribes,** including the Natchez, Choctaw, and Creek. These tribes were more likely, for example, to have a chief or king who had strong personal authority over the tribe. Indians who lived farther to the east and north were more likely to have a system of government based on a greater sharing of power.

BINDING TIES

Apr 8, 1914
J 191658

Family and community relationships were central to the lives of the Indians of eastern North America. A person's ties to other members of the **tribe** affected everything he or she did.

Clans

The **clan** was the building block of the community among the Indians of the Northeast and the Southeast. A clan was a group of people who were connected to each other through family ties. In most cases, members of a clan shared a common ancestor, sometimes an ancestor many generations back. There were exceptions, however. A person might join a clan through marriage or adoption.

Clan relationships were very close. Clan members were expected to show loyalty and to defend other members of the clan against all enemies. Marriage within the clan was forbidden. Even though two members of a clan might not actually share a blood tie, they could not marry each other.

In the Northeast, the Iroquois recognized nine clans. These were the bear, wolf, turtle, deer, eel, beaver, hawk, heron, and **snipe**. They believed that each clan had the characteristics of the animal for which it was named. In Iroquois villages, several families belonging to the same clan might share a large home.

Each Iroquois clan was headed by a clan mother, who performed a number of important roles. Clan mothers were responsible for making sure that children were raised to respect Iroquois traditions. They gave clan names to the children. They also chose the clan chiefs, who would represent the clan in the Iroquois Grand Council.

▲ A panoramic photograph of Iroquois Indians taken in 1914 in Buffalo, New York. The people in the photo were possibly members of a single clan. The clan, that is, a community of people who share a common ancestor, was central to the **culture** of Eastern North American Indians.

ANIMALS OF EARTH, AIR AND WATER

The Iroquois viewed their various clan animals as creatures of the earth, air, or water. The turtle, beaver, and eel were water animals; the deer, wolf, and bear were earth animals; and the hawk, heron, and snipe belonged to the air. By associating clan animals with the natural elements, the Iroquois were expressing their belief that all things in the natural world are interconnected.

In the Southeast, the Cherokee and Seminole also had an extended clan system. The names of the clans have changed over the course of these tribes' history. However, the relationships defined by the clans remains the same. Like the Iroquois, the Cherokee and Seminole took many clan names from animals.

Blood Lines

Most of the Indians of the Northeast and the Southeast, including the Iroquois, Cherokee, and Seminole, had a **matrilineal** society. According to this system, a child belonged to his or her mother's clan, and clan membership was traced back through the mother's ancestors.

Some of the northeastern Algonquian tribes, however, were **patrilineal**. These tribes traced an individual's **lineage** (*LIHN ee ihj*) through his or her father's ancestors. Children belonged to the father's clan.

INDIAN SOCIETY

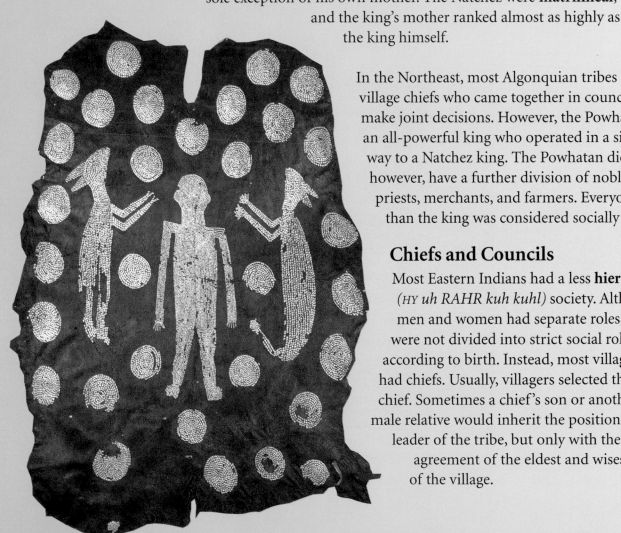

▼ Chief Powhatan's deerskin mantle (cloak) is decorated with a human silhouette, hare and turtle figures, and shell patterns. Powhatan was the all-powerful chief of the Powhatan people of Virginia. Strongly opposed to friendly relations with European colonists, he formed a confederacy with neighboring Algonquian tribes.

The Indians of the Northeast and the Southeast had well-developed systems of government. Across these two cultural areas, societies were arranged in one of two ways. One arrangement divided people strictly according to their position in society. The other arrangement was less rigid and gave people a greater say in how they were governed.

To Be a King

A few Southeast Indian **tribes** had rigid social systems. For the Natchez, social rank was extremely important. The king and his relatives occupied the highest rank. Immediately below were **nobles** and priests. Merchants came next in order, with farmers at the bottom.

A Natchez king had total control over the people below him. He could make life-and-death decisions about other tribe members—with the sole exception of his own mother. The Natchez were **matrilineal**, and the king's mother ranked almost as highly as the king himself.

In the Northeast, most Algonquian tribes had village chiefs who came together in councils to make joint decisions. However, the Powhatan had an all-powerful king who operated in a similar way to a Natchez king. The Powhatan did not, however, have a further division of nobles, priests, merchants, and farmers. Everyone other than the king was considered socially equal.

Chiefs and Councils

Most Eastern Indians had a less **hierarchical** (HY uh RAHR kuh kuhl) society. Although men and women had separate roles, people were not divided into strict social roles according to birth. Instead, most villages had chiefs. Usually, villagers selected their chief. Sometimes a chief's son or another male relative would inherit the position of leader of the tribe, but only with the agreement of the eldest and wisest people of the village.

▲ Shawnee leaders meet in council. For a confederacy to succeed, the leaders of the different tribes had to negotiate with each other. Together they made decisions that would benefit the whole confederacy, not just a particular tribe.

Indian Confederacies

In the Northeast and the Southeast, groups of tribes formed **confederacies.** By grouping together, tribes could support one another when necessary. In addition to the most famous example, the Iroquois Confederacy, some Algonquian tribes also formed confederacies. The Powhatan, for instance, formed a confederacy with some neighboring Algonquian tribes. Another, the Abenaki Confederacy, was based in present-day Maine and included several Algonquian tribes. In the Southeast, the Creek Confederacy was the largest and most powerful grouping. The Seminole tribe formed in the 1700's when it broke off from the Creek Confederacy.

CLAN MOTHERS

Among the Iroquois, the **clan** mothers selected the chiefs. A village might have a number of chiefs who would meet in councils to make decisions concerning the village. Although women could not speak in the chiefs' councils, women had councils of their own. The Iroquois clan mothers had an important right: if their council decided that the chief was not doing a good job, the clan mothers could order him to step down.

LEADERS WHO MADE A DIFFERENCE

The Peacemaker

According to Iroquois tradition, the Iroquoian **tribes** feuded and fought with one another during their early history. Around the early 1500's a man named Deganawida *(deh gah nah WEE dah)* became concerned that continual infighting would destroy the Iroquois. Deganawida believed that the Iroquois tribes should put aside their differences. He argued that they should focus their war efforts against outside enemies, not one another. By grouping together, the Iroquois might become a unified, strong, and prosperous people.

Deganawida joined with Hiawatha *(hy uh WAH thuh)*, a well-known warrior and **medicine man.** Together, the two men traveled among the Iroquois tribes and spread their idea of unity and peace. This campaign earned Deganawida the name Peacemaker. Eventually his idea took root, and the Cayuga, Mohawk, Oneida, Onondaga, and Seneca came together to form the Iroquois Confederacy, also known as the Five Nations. In the 1720's, after the Tuscarora *(TUHS kuh RAWR uh)* joined, the group became known as the Six Nations.

ELY SAMUEL PARKER
In the 1820's, the United States created the Bureau of Indian Affairs to deal with the Indians, but conflict continued to escalate as people of European descent kept moving west. In 1869, President Ulysses S. Grant appointed Ely Samuel Parker (right), a Seneca Iroquois, to serve as the first Native American head of the bureau. Because Parker defended Indian rights and Indians trusted him, violence between settlers and Indians declined during his term as commissioner.

◀ *Osceola* by the American painter George Catlin (1796-1872). Osceola's commitment to keep the Seminole people free of the control of the U.S. government impressed both friends and enemies alike. His intelligence was legendary, and he usually managed to escape from U.S. troops sent to capture him. Counties in Florida and Iowa are named for the Seminole chief.

Osceola

The Seminole tribe formed in the 1700's as an offshoot of the Creek nations of present-day Georgia and Alabama. The Seminole wanted to put themselves out of reach of the Europeans (chiefly the British and Spanish) who were beginning to colonize the Southeast. (The tribe's name, *Seminole*, means *runaways* in the Creek language.)

The greatest Seminole leader, Osceola *(OS ee OH luh)*, spent his life trying to win freedom for his tribe from outside control. Osceola tried to keep his people out of conflict with the United States, but U.S. settlers wanted Seminole land, and Osceola refused to give it up. He fought hard against the removal of the Seminole from Florida to lands farther west. In 1838, the U.S. Army captured Osceola during a truce. Even at the time, this betrayal met with widespread disapproval. Osceola died three months later. He remains a hero for the Seminole people.

Beloved Woman

Nancy Ward was a Cherokee who lived in the 1700's. Her name is an Americanized version of her Indian name, Nanye-hi *(NAN yeh hee)*. In 1775, her husband, Kingfisher, was killed during a battle against the Creek Indians. Nanye-hi took his musket and continued to fire it, helping the Cherokee win the battle. In her honor, the tribe awarded her the title Beloved Woman and gave her a voice in the tribal council. She also had the power to save from death captives taken in battle. In the 1780's, Nancy Ward was active in peace negotiations between settlers and the Cherokee. Later, she advised against allowing more settlers onto Cherokee land.

WAR

For many of the Indians of the Northeast and Southeast cultural areas, war was an ever-present fact of life. Generally speaking, all able-bodied men were expected to be ready for war at all times. Indians of eastern North America waged war against their rivals for purposes of revenge, self-defense, to test their strength and bravery, and occasionally for other reasons, even mourning.

Mourning Wars

The Iroquois **tribes** had a tradition of fighting a mourning war. The Iroquois fought these wars to make up for the loss of a loved one. The loved one might have died in battle or as a result of disease or some other misfortune.

The goal of the mourning war was to take captives who could be adopted into the tribe as replacements for whoever had died. First, the Iroquois tribe raided a neighboring tribe and took prisoners. These prisoners were then forced to undergo an **ordeal.** One ordeal—"running the gauntlet"— involved running between two rows of people who would all beat the runner with sticks, fists, or feet.

Those captives who made it through the ordeal then took part in a great feast. After the feast, the female relatives of the person who had died decided whether or not to adopt a captive and give him or her the family's name. Rejected captives faced further torture and were eventually killed. A rejected captive who had demonstrated exceptional bravery might be eaten. The Iroquois believed that the person's bravery passed to anyone who ate his flesh.

▲ A tomahawk *(TOM uh hawk)*, the most common weapon used by Eastern Indians, dating from the 1700's. The iron head is etched with a scene of an Indian attacking a European settler. Before the arrival of Europeans in North America, the heads of tomahawks were made of stone.

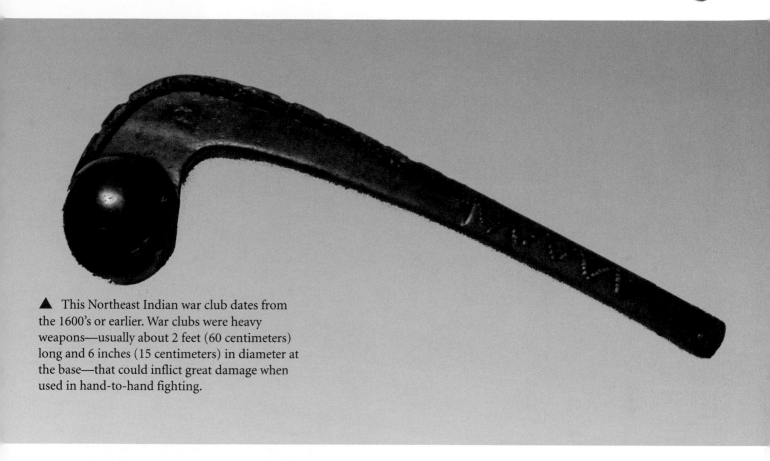

▲ This Northeast Indian war club dates from the 1600's or earlier. War clubs were heavy weapons—usually about 2 feet (60 centimeters) long and 6 inches (15 centimeters) in diameter at the base—that could inflict great damage when used in hand-to-hand fighting.

The Iroquois fought so many mourning wars that they were almost always at war. The desire to end this tradition was one of Deganawida's main motives when he urged the Iroquois to unify. With the formation of the Iroquois **Confederacy,** the mourning wars among Iroquois tribes stopped.

War and Peace Divisions

The Southeast Indians lived in areas where there were more than enough resources for everyone. Therefore, they did not usually fight wars to take new territory. Primarily, they fought wars to test their warriors' skill and courage. The ability to face great challenges and overcome great dangers was a mark of honor.

Members of such tribes as the Cherokee and Creek divided themselves into two categories: red, representing war matters; and white, representing peace matters. The "red" warriors kept themselves in readiness for battle in much the same way as a modern athlete keeps in shape. The "white" organization handled community affairs during peacetime. Among the Creek, there were separate "white" and "red" towns.

WAR WOMAN
The Cherokee allowed certain women to follow the warriors to the battlefield. A War Woman did not usually take part in the fighting, though there were times when she might take up her slain husband's weapon and continue fighting. The main role of the War Woman was to help injured warriors off the battlefield and to treat wounds. The War Woman also had responsibility for deciding which captives would live and which would die.

THE ROLES OF MEN AND WOMEN

There were significant differences between the way of life of the northeastern and southeastern **tribes.** Yet the way Indians of the two **culture** groups divided work between men and women was similar. This was especially true in areas where farming was a major part of everyday life.

A Man's Responsibilities

In both the Northeast and the Southeast, men were responsible for chores and duties away from the home. The men hunted and fished for food. Among the Iroquois, the men cut down the trees that were used to build walls around the villages. They also built large, rectangular dwellings called **longhouses.** Some longhouses were more than 100 feet (30 meters) in length.

A man was responsible for defending his village and his family from attack and, when necessary, for launching an attack on an enemy village. Men not only made war but also made the weapons for war—clubs and javelins, for example. The men of a village also made such specialized hunting tools as blowguns and darts.

A Woman's Life

In Eastern Indian society, as in most American Indian societies, women were responsible for the family's daily needs. They looked after the home, made clothes, cooked food, and took care of small children. Among the Iroquois and Cherokee, the home and the garden belonged to the woman of the family.

▲ A Powhatan man carries an arrow **quiver** made from deerskin and deer fur and wears a **tunic** made from **tanned** deerskin. Hunting was an important part of life for any Eastern Indian man. Game, especially deer, was plentiful in the northeastern and southeastern woodlands. Indians ate deer meat and used the skins for shelter and clothing.

CHILD'S PLAY

The Northeast and Southeast Indians encouraged children to explore and play but also expected them to learn the skills they would need as adults. Indian children spent much of their time learning. Young boys hunted such small animals as birds and squirrels. They helped the men fish or build dwellings and boats. Girls helped the women gather plants and grow crops. Young girls learned the basics of sewing and decorating clothing by watching their mothers and grandmothers.

Raising crops was primarily the responsibility of women. They made decisions about what crops to plant and when to plant them. Women then tended the crops and harvested them when they were ready. Women also butchered the meat the men brought in. Some of the meat might be eaten right away; the women preserved and stored the rest.

Shared Tasks

Among the Indians of the Northeast and the Southeast, men and women participated together in a range of pastimes. These included such entertainments as storytelling, music, and art. Men usually made sacred masks used in religious **rituals** and at special festivals. Women created elaborate beadwork and **quillwork**. Both men and women studied the medical uses of herbs and plants.

▶ A young Cherokee woman carries her child while fishing in a 1942 photograph. Eastern Indian women were responsible for tending food crops but might also help with fishing or trapping small animals.

LAW OF THE PEOPLE

Indians of the Northeast and Southeast based their legal systems on both tradition and common sense. The handling of certain traditions, such as marriage, differed from **tribe** to tribe. However, there is a remarkable similarity in the way tribes across both **culture** groups handled major crimes.

Crime and Punishment

A powerful sense of kinship and loyalty held Indian societies together. As a result, a violent action that hurt one person was seen as hurting all members of the tribe. Murder was considered the worst of all crimes because it deprived the tribe of a person when the tribe needed as many people as possible to remain strong.

There was no police force or legal system to punish people who committed serious crimes. Instead, it was usually left to the families or **clans** of victims of crime to punish offenders.

Crime Within the Clan

The killing of one member of a clan by another member of the same clan was viewed as a family matter among the Iroquois and Cherokee. The killer was usually not sentenced to death, as the tribe's goal was to prevent further

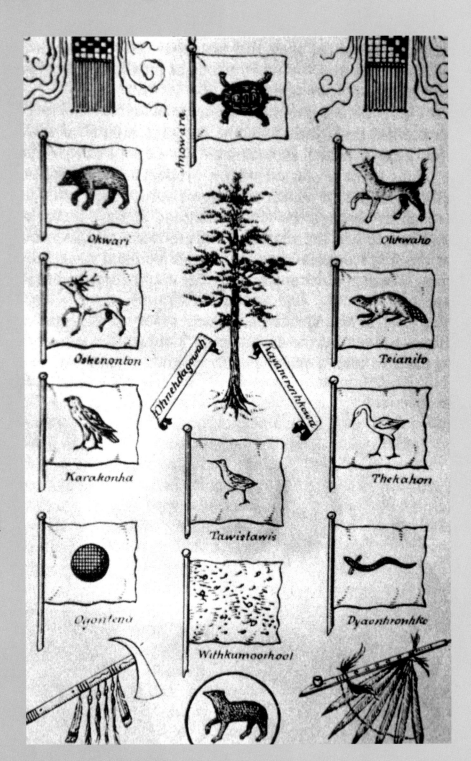

▲ A drawing of the various Iroquois clan animals from the 1700's. Clans could seek revenge against people who harmed clan members.

◀ Furs were highly prized among the Indians of the Northeast. A clan that had offended another clan within a tribe might make amends by publicly offering a batch of furs as a gift.

bloodshed. Instead, the clan required the criminal to make amends for the crime. The clan elders decided what form those amends would take. The clan could, in extreme cases, **banish** the offender. This punishment essentially amounted to a sentence of death; a person would be unlikely to survive long separated from the protection of the clan.

In other cases, a criminal might be shamed in front of the entire village or tribe. Members of the tribe would publicly scorn the criminal and announce that he no longer deserved to be called a brother or a friend. He would be compared to the most despised enemies. In a society that valued respect from others and personal honor, shame was a strong punishment.

Crime Between Clans

If someone committed a violent crime against a member of a different clan, it was vital to work out a punishment that would satisfy the wronged party. Iroquois tribes recognized that punishing a murderer with the death sentence was a bad idea in such cases. Taking a life for a life might spark a cycle of revenge between clans that would hurt the tribe as a whole. Instead, the offending clan might offer payments or gifts to make up for the loss of life. The offering of payments or such gifts as furs, which were highly valued by the Northeastern Indians, took place in a formal council in front of the chiefs and elders of the tribe. It was an important **ritual** that was meant to heal the wounds of sorrow and anger for the good of the whole tribe.

SCARS TELL A STORY
Among the Seminole, a person who had committed a serious crime might receive a physical punishment that took the form of scarring. Deep cuts were made on the criminal's arms or legs. The scars that remained after the cuts healed reminded everyone who saw them of the person's crime. Scarring was not always an indicator of a serious crime, though. Sometimes a person chose to scar himself or herself when mourning a loved one or reflecting on a lost battle.

LIVING WITH THE SPIRITS

Accounts of the origin of the world and of animals and people differed from **tribe** to tribe in the Northeast and Southeast cultural areas. Yet certain core beliefs were common to all tribes.

The Indians of the Northeast and Southeast, like all American Indians, believed that human life was influenced by spirits. They believed that some of these spirits were guides that could help a person lead a good life. Other evil or harmful spirits were the causes of illness and conflict.

A World of Spirits

The Indians believed that plants, animals, water, and even rocks and mountains all had their own life force, or spirit. These spirits were sources of wisdom. Those who knew how to communicate with them could learn valuable lessons from them.

▲ An Ojibwa hand drum with a painted deerskin head. Medicine men used drums in many ceremonies and rituals. During a healing song, a healer might beat an accompaniment on the drum. Indians also believed that rhythmic beating on the drumhead helped a medicine man to communicate with spirits.

A Constant Presence

The spirits influenced the world of people at all times. Certain spirits could help ensure a successful hunt. Other spirits helped the corn grow tall and strong. There were spirits that played tricks on people and spirits that disliked people enough to wish to harm them. Certain Algonquian tribes of the Northeast believed in Windigo, a cruel and dangerous spirit that enjoyed causing people harm.

The Indians believed that the spirits appreciated gifts. For example, if a hunter wanted help finding deer, he might leave a bit of tobacco on the ground to persuade a spirit to help him. Family members might make an offering of corn or herbs to encourage an angry spirit to leave the body of a sick person and allow him or her to get well.

Medicine men

Most tribes had one or more people who were considered to have special powers. These people were called **medicine men** or medicine women. It was believed that these healers knew how to speak directly to the many spirits of the world. They used their knowledge of herbs to cure the sick and performed **rituals** to guarantee a good harvest.

Secret Medicine Societies

Many tribes in the Northeast had secret medicine societies, an organization for healers. One such group was the Midewiwin *(mee DAY wee wihn)*. Members were considered especially skilled at curing illness. They recorded their secret rituals and remedies by using sharpened bone to cut symbols on birchbark scrolls. The scrolls could then be sent to other Midewiwin Society members many miles away.

THE STORY OF DIRTY CLOTHES

In one Iroquois story, a young boy called Dirty Clothes shared his food with the Little People, or Jo-Ge-Oh. The Jo-Ge-Oh then taught the boy about useful plants and about the ways of the forest animals. They also taught the boy a special dance. The boy carried this valuable information back to his tribe. In gratitude, the Indians performed the dance, called the Dark Dance. This dance was performed at night, when the Jo-Ge-Oh could join in without being seen.

▲ Chippewa picture-writing on a birchbark scroll. The scroll records a sacred song that may have been used in a Midewiwin ritual. Medicine men also recorded remedies for diseases on pieces of birchbark. Pictures might describe the herbs or other materials needed to cure a certain illness.

HEALTH AND MEDICINE

The **medicine man** had two major duties: looking after the spiritual well-being of the **tribe**; and keeping people in good physical health. Medicine men and medicine women had special knowledge of the medicines and **rituals** that Indians believed cured illness. For the Indians of eastern North America, medicine and spirituality were closely connected.

Controlling the Spirits

Many of the eastern tribes believed that animal or plant spirits directly caused illness. They believed that it was possible to control these spirits with certain rituals. The purpose of these rituals was either to drive out bad spirits or to invite good spirits in.

In the Southeast, the Cherokee believed that certain animal spirits had invented diseases. The diseases were the spirits' way of getting revenge on the people who had hurt or killed the animals they represented. To fight a disease, a Cherokee medicine man worked out a formula of magical charms, songs, and herbal medicines to drive away the

HONORING THE PAST

The sacred medicine masks of the Iroquois have long been considered works of art. Many museums as well as individuals collected the unique, handmade masks. The Iroquois, however, view the masks as special beings that must not be displayed, sold, photographed, or drawn. They believe that only members of the Iroquois medicine societies have the authority and right to care for the masks. In 1995, Chief Leon Shenandoah of the Iroquois tribe's Grand Council asked that all medicine masks be returned. In 1998, the National Museum of the American Indian in New York City (since relocated to Washington, D.C.) became one of the first public organizations to honor this request. The museum authorities returned all of the medicine masks that they had displayed or stored. Since then, many other museums have returned masks to the Iroquois.

◀ An engraving from around 1850 depicts an Algonquian shaman (medicine man) making medicine inside a mat-covered wigwam *(WIHG wom)*. While mixing ingredients, he shakes a gourd rattle and chants to increase the medicine's effectiveness.

animal spirits. He might also try to understand an illness by asking the patient about his or her dreams.

In the Northeast, Iroquois medicine men treated illness in sacred healing ceremonies. During these ceremonies, the medicine man wore a wooden mask that had been carved from a living tree. Only those who belonged to sacred medicine societies could make the masks. No two masks were alike, and the Iroquois believed that each had its own spirit and power.

Plants and Herbs

The Eastern Indians treated both simple and serious illnesses using the many plants and herbs that grew in the forests. They used tree bark, roots, stems, leaves, and blossoms in different ways to help a sick patient recover. The plants and herbs might be made into a **poultice** *(POHL tihs)*, a heated mixture of medicine that was placed on the skin. It was also common to boil herbs and plants to make a kind of tea. Medicine men often treated headaches by making a tea from willow bark. Scientists have since discovered that willow bark contains the chemical that is used to make aspirin, a modern headache remedy.

◀ A carved wooden figure that was used by members of the Midewiwin medicine society to carry birchbark scrolls from camp to camp.

HONORING LIFE AND DEATH

Ceremonies were a central feature of life for the Indians of the Northeast and the Southeast. In ceremonies, Indians celebrated important events in life and marked the death of loved ones. Ceremonies also helped to create a sense of community among the people of the **tribe.** Some ceremonies were common to almost all eastern tribes. Others were specific to a certain tribe or region.

First New Moon of Spring

Most Indians—especially those who lived in colder climates—performed some kind of ceremony to welcome the spring. The Cherokee celebrated the first new moon of spring in March. Their ceremony welcomed the new leaves just appearing on the trees. It was a celebration of life and lasted seven days. During the seven-day festival, there was dancing, and a person called the Fire Maker tended the Sacred Fire. The fires that burned in people's homes were extinguished and then re-lit with a coal or brand from the Sacred Fire. This act celebrated the unity of the tribe.

▼ A Seminole Green Corn Dance, at which Seminoles from different camps came together to give thanks and celebrate. The long line of people around the central fire are stomp dancing. The man at the front of the line holding the feather fan is the **medicine man,** the dance leader. As he chants, the male dancers stomp their feet in rhythm, while the female dancers make a quieter sound by shuffling their feet along the ground. Many Eastern Indian tribes held a version of the Green Corn Ceremony.

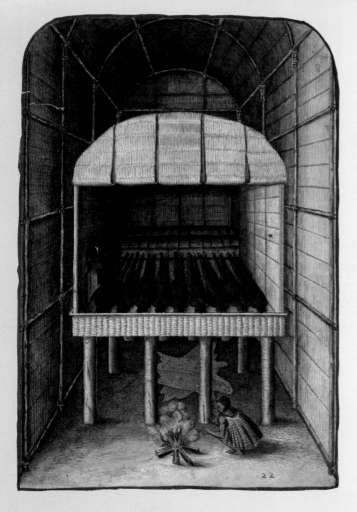

◀ An Algonquian tomb of Weroans, or chief lords, in a 1590 engraving by Theodor de Bry. Some of the Algonquian tribes in Virginia and the Carolinas built special tombs for their chiefs. When a chief died, his body was prepared in a **ritual** and then laid next to other chiefs' bodies on a platform in the tomb. The fire dried out the bodies as a way of preserving them.

Green Corn Ceremony

Corn was an important food for Indians in eastern North America. When the first corn ripened in late summer, many Eastern Indian tribes held a festival known as the Green Corn Ceremony. The ceremony involved not only roasting the early corn in its husk and eating it but also a period of **fasting**. Those taking part in the ceremony offered prayers of thanks and celebrated with dancing and singing. In the Southeast, among the Choctaw and Cherokee, the various activities of the Green Corn Ceremony lasted for several days.

Feast of the Dead

The Huron were an Iroquoian tribe who once lived in what is now central Ontario, Canada. Every 10 to 12 years, the Huron held a special ceremony called the Feast of the Dead. The purpose of this ceremony was to pay tribute to members of the tribe who had died since the last Feast of the Dead. The remains of these people were taken from the cemetery and brought to the village. The villagers danced and feasted to honor the dead people's spirits. When the feast ended, the dead were reburied in a single large pit.

HOUSE OF THE DEAD

When a Choctaw died, tribespeople left the body exposed to the sun and allowed it to dry out and decay. The Choctaw believed that this practice allowed the spirit of the deceased to rejoin the sun, which they considered to be a supreme power.

The body was then dressed in what had been the person's best clothing and decorated with body paint. After about a year, a member of the Turkey Buzzard Society scraped the bones clean with his long fingernails. Then, without first cleaning his nails, the bone picker prepared a feast of meat, corn, and other vegetables for the entire village. When the feast was over, the deceased person's bones were wrapped and taken to the bone-house, where they were either hung or placed on a shelf.

USEFUL ART

Like other North American Indians, the Eastern Indian **tribes** made useful objects from natural materials. They used wood, plant fibers, mineral dyes, and animal products to create the items they needed every day, such as baskets, boxes, arrow **quivers**, and **cradleboards**. Although such items served practical purposes, many were also beautifully made.

Art in Wood

The peoples of the Northeast and the Southeast made great use of the trees that grew in the areas they inhabited. They cut thin strips of birch, elm, yellow pine, and other wood and wove these strips into baskets. They used these baskets to carry loads around or to store goods in the home.

▶ A Huron comb and pouch dating from the 1600's. The comb is carved from deer antler. The pouch is woven from hemp, a fibrous plant, and is decorated with embroidered deer hair.

The Indians of the Northeast used the bark of the birch tree for making a wide range of domestic items, including storage boxes, dishes, water buckets, and even cooking pots. They made containers for holding water or cooking food by cutting and bending pieces of birchbark into the desired shape and sealing them with pine pitch. The pine pitch prevented liquid from leaking out of the container. Birchbark absorbs water, which would leave the bottom of a cooking pot damp enough to prevent it from burning on the fire.

Northeastern Indians made beautiful storage boxes from different woods. These boxes were often decorated with animal, flower, or geometric design patterns. Sometimes the box maker also stained the wood with paint made from crushed minerals and water.

▼ A Menominee box made of birchbark (center) decorated with porcupine quills (right).

Woven Wonders

In the Southeast, Cherokee and Chitimacha (*chiht ee MAH cha*) women wove baskets that had two walls. The double wall made the baskets very strong and, therefore, suitable for carrying heavy loads. Some baskets were decorated with shells or painted with berry juice.

A woman's designs were considered her personal property. A design was a form of signature and could not be used by another person. Sometimes, however, a weaver could make a gift of a design to a close friend or relative.

Modeling with Clay

Some Southeast Indians, such as the Cherokee, made pots and other containers from clay. They made clay pots by hand by forming the clay into a ball and then pushing it into a rough bowl shape with their fingers and hands. They then beat the outside with a paddle to form the exact shape they wanted. They decorated pots with carved designs, feathers, or sticks while the clay was still wet. They then baked the pots in ovens to make them hard and durable. These sturdy pots were used as food storage containers inside the home and also as decorative objects outdoors.

RECORDING HISTORY

The Cherokee developed a written version of their language in the 1800's. Eastern Indians used methods other than writing to record important events or to communicate important messages. The **wampum** *(WOM puhm)* belt was one of the most common methods.

White Shell Beads

The word *wampum* derives from an Algonquian word meaning *white shell beads*. The Algonquian **tribes** and other Indians of eastern North America made white beads from **whelk** (sea snail) shells and purple beads from clamshells. Craftspeople used sharp stone drills to make holes

WAMPUM CONSTITUTION

The Great Binding Law, or **Constitution,** of the Iroquois Confederacy was recorded on 114 wampum belts. The constitution itself described the number of strings of wampum that certain situations required. For example, a man being elected to the Great Council had to provide four strings of wampum to the Council as representatives of the Iroquois people. This donation proved that he was committed to his role as an Iroquois chief.

▼ Wampum beads were made from the purple and white shells of clams and whelks. The hole in each bead had to be carefully drilled by hand to avoid breaking the shell. Because the beads were difficult to make, wampum had great value as trade items. Wampum were also used during ceremonies and worn by important members of the tribe.

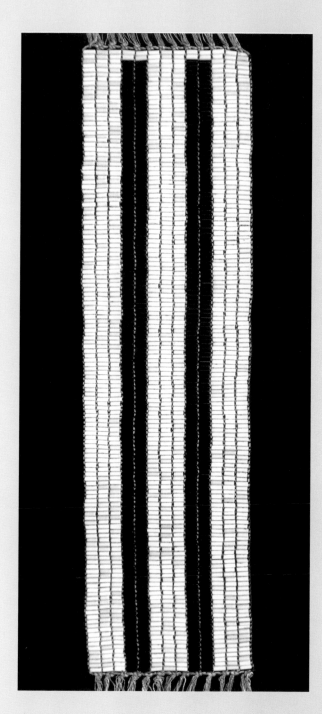

▲ A belt called the Two Row Wampum, which records a treaty between the Iroquois and Dutch colonists in 1613. The white beads symbolize truth and peace. The purple rows represent the paths of the Europeans and the Indians, who agree to follow their own laws without getting in each other's way.

in the beads, then polished the beads with sand. They threaded the wampum onto long strings of twisted plant fibers or animal tendons. They then wove together the strings of beads to make belts.

Most belts were not wide. They usually had no more than seven strings of shells and measured from 2 to 6 feet (60 to 180 centimeters) long.

Words in Beads

Although wampum could be merely decorative, it usually had a more important purpose. Indians used wampum to remember special events and to conduct the tribe's official business. A wampum belt might signify a peace treaty or a trade agreement between tribes. Such major Indian **confederacies** as the Creek and Cherokee in the Southeast and the Iroquois in the Northeast used wampum for a wide range of official purposes.

Many Indian peoples had a messenger or speaker who was specially trained to "read" wampum belts. This person was able to tell the story contained in the beads to an assembly of the tribe or to a council of leaders. In some Cherokee towns, the people gathered every year to hear a speaker recite the laws of the tribe while holding sacred wampum belts.

Trading with Wampum

In the 1600's, some European merchants used wampum as a form of money when trading with Indians. Europeans might give wampum in exchange for furs or other Indian goods. For the Indians, though, the wampum also had great spiritual and ceremonial importance. Only wampum made by hand in the traditional manner had the highest value. European traders began mass-producing wampum beads, but Indians considered these beads of inferior quality and, therefore, of lower value.

VILLAGES AND TOWNS

Most of the Indians of the Northeast and the Southeast lived in permanent or semi-permanent villages. With a relatively settled pattern of life, they were able to maintain large community gardens. In these gardens, they grew an assortment of food.

Staying in One Place

Villages and towns were usually located close to a river or lake. Nearby were cleared fields where the women planted and tended the vegetables and fruits on which the **tribe** depended for survival. Also nearby were woods in which the men hunted.

Some small villages consisted of just a few dwellings. Seminole villages, for example, often contained just a few houses. On the other hand, some Iroquois villages had 50 or more houses. A village this size could be home to several hundred people. Such a large village might remain in place for 15 or 20 years. The residents farmed the soil until it was no longer **fertile** and hunted until it became too difficult to find game. At that point, they dismantled the village and moved to a new location.

Protection from Enemies

Some Iroquois and Cherokee villages were built within tall walls called palisades *(PAL uh SAYDZ).* A palisade was made by driving logs into the ground then binding the logs together to form a thick and sturdy barrier. Sometimes, other logs were laid horizontally across the top to form a walkway. From this walkway, lookouts had a clear view of approaching enemies.

◀ An Algonquian village in North Carolina in a sketch made in 1585 by the English explorer John White. A tall log palisade protects the **long-houses** and wigwams from unfriendly invaders.

The Natchez built towns that were unlike those built by any other group in the Northeast or Southeast. More like small cities than villages, a Natchez town could cover an area as large as several square miles and could house many thousands of people. Many Natchez towns were surrounded by fences of sharp stakes.

Shared Structures

Permanent or semipermanent Iroquois and Cherokee villages usually included a number of community buildings—places that everyone in the village shared. Indians used these buildings for councils, ceremonies, and other special occasions. Some were quite large; an Iroquois village might have a council hall that was more than 200 feet (60 meters) long. Cherokee often held their ceremonies in large seven-sided buildings.

Many Cherokee villages also had a sports field for playing **lacrosse** *(luh KRAWS)*. Spectators could watch this lively and popular game from benches built along the sides of the field.

▲ An illustration depicts daily life among the Indians who lived in the region of Lake Ontario. Villages were the heart of tribal life for all eastern Indians. Most had at least one community building— a large longhouse, for example—and numerous family houses. Some villages were enclosed within tall log palisades to provide greater protection from attacking enemies. The walkway along the top of the palisade also allowed villagers to keep an eye on their crop fields.

SUMMER HOMES

Some Cherokee tribes moved between two villages. One was used during the winter months, and the other during the summer. The summer homes were located near large cleared fields in which farmers grew a variety of crops. The people stayed in the summer homes until harvest time, when they moved back to the winter village. Homes in the winter village offered protection from the cold weather.

SHELTERS

Indians of the Northeast and the Southeast built their dwellings from materials that they had available to them in their surroundings, primarily tree branches and bark. Their houses needed to provide comfort and shelter and suit the particular climate in which a **tribe** lived.

Longhouses

The Iroquois tribes called themselves the Haudenosaunee *(hoh dee noh SHOH nee)*, which means *we* **longhouse** *builders*. The longhouse was the type of dwelling most commonly used by the Iroquois and some of their neighbors in the Northeast cultural area.

A longhouse consisted of a frame of wooden poles covered with sheets of elm bark. A typical longhouse measured 50 to 100 feet (15 to 30 meters) in length, but some longhouses were up to 200 feet (60 meters) long.

Each longhouse was home to several families belonging to the same **clan**. With up to 60 people (and sometimes their dogs) sharing one longhouse, life indoors could be noisy and crowded.

▼ A wigwam typical of those built by Iroquois tribes. The structure consisted of bent saplings covered with panels of bark.

▲ A settlement of Seminole chickees in Florida.

The Iroquois used wood screens and mats to divide longhouses into separate rooms. As a result, each family had its own space within the shared dwelling. Raised platforms ran along the inside walls of the longhouse. These platforms provided space for sleeping. Each longhouse also had several fires for cooking and warmth. Holes in the roof allowed some of the smoke to escape, but it was often smoky inside a longhouse.

Birchbark Houses

Northeastern Indians also lived in wigwams. A wigwam was a small house, around 8 to 10 feet (250 to 300 centimeters) tall. It consisted of a wooden frame covered with large pieces of birchbark. Most wigwams were either rectangular with an arched roof or circular with a domed roof. Some wigwams were constructed in the shape of a cone. A wigwam was large enough to serve as a comfortable home for several months at a time and was designed to be quickly assembled.

Unlike the Iroquois, the Algonquian tribes usually had a summer camp and a winter hunting camp. When the season changed, the residents of an entire village moved together to a new location and built new wigwams.

Homes for a Warm Climate

The climate of the Southeast was warmer than the Northeast. Southeastern Indians' dwellings reflected this environmental difference. The Cherokee, for example, built houses of **wattle and daub**. They made these houses by weaving flexible strips of wood and vines onto a wooden frame. They then covered the woven areas with a mud plaster that would dry thoroughly in the warm climate. They made roofs from thatched grass or bark.

In Florida, the Seminole built distinctive houses called chickees. A chickee consisted of posts supporting a thatched roof and a wooden platform. The house was raised several feet off the ground to prevent it from sinking into the swampy soil and to keep out snakes and other pests. A chickee was open on all sides to take advantage of breezes. In rainy weather, the Seminole lashed thin mats of grasses or animal hide to the chickee's frame to keep out water.

CLOTHING AND DECORATION

Indians adapted their clothing to suit the season. During the warm summer months, most of the Indians of the Northeast and the Southeast wore little clothing.

Everyday Wear

The **breechcloth** was the most common item of summer clothing for men and boys of the northeastern and southeastern **tribes.** Also called a loincloth, a breechcloth is a long rectangle of deerskin or a similar soft material. The wearer placed it between the legs and looped the excess cloth at the front and back over a belt. By leaving the legs bare, a breechcloth kept the body cool in hot weather.

During the winter months, Indians might wear a breechcloth together with a pair of deerskin leggings that also attached to the belt. On the upper body, men and boys wore a deerskin **tunic** or shirt and perhaps a fur-lined cloak if the weather was very cold. In the Southeast, winter often brought rain. In rainy conditions, Indians might wear a deerskin cloak or a woven **poncho** to stay dry.

Women wore a wrap-around skirt or tunic made of **tanned** deerskin. Some Iroquois women also wore shorter leggings under the skirt. In the Southeast, some skirts were made from woven plant fibers. Men and women alike wore deerskin **moccasins.** During the winter months, Indians living in the colder Northeast might wear moccasins lined with rabbit or squirrel fur.

Body Art

Tattoos were a common form of body decoration among many of the tribes of the Northeast and Southeast. The Cherokee and

▼ A drawing from the 1500's depicts a heavily tattooed Timucua *(tih MOO kwah)* Indian of Florida wearing a breechcloth and a **pendant.** The **quiver** on his back contains arrows for his bow.

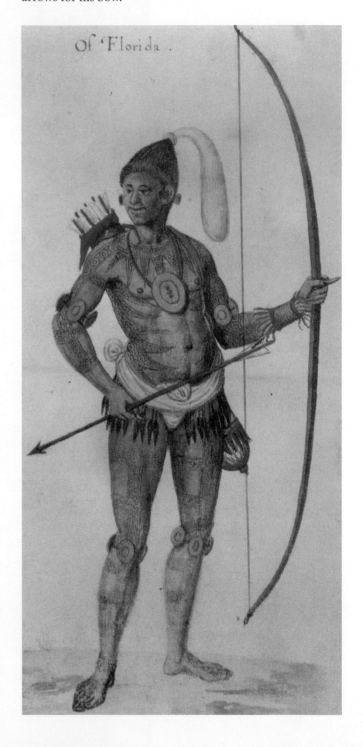

Of Florida.

◀ A young Mohawk, photographed in Montreal, Canada, performs a tribal dance wearing a traditional sleeveless deerskin tunic. On his head, he wears a roach decorated with feathers.

Iroquois were especially known for the detail and complexity of their tattoos. Some Choctaw men covered almost their entire bodies with tattoos. Usually only the men wore tattoos, though some Seminole women also had simple tattoos. Tattoo designs often incorporated **clan** symbols.

Indians made tattoos by first cutting the skin with sharp pieces of bone, shell, or stone, and then rubbing soot or plant dyes into the cuts. Although similar to modern tattooing techniques, the Indian method was far more painful. The ability to bear such pain without showing discomfort was seen as a sign of bravery.

ROACHES

A roach is a headdress that was traditionally worn by the men of various eastern tribes, often into battle. Dancers still wear roaches. By adding a roach to his own hair, a man made his appearance dramatic and sometimes fierce.

The roach was made from stiff animal hair. Moose hair and porcupine quills were especially popular. Indians attached the animal hair to a base made from leather or bone in such a way that the hair protruded straight from the wearer's head, much like a crest. They often dyed the roach bright colors and decorated it with feathers or shells.

Many Eastern Indian men shaved the whole head except for one lock of hair, which formed a natural roach on top of the head. This hairstyle is sometimes called a mohawk after the tribe with which it is associated.

TRANSPORTATION

The Indians who inhabited eastern North America lived near many rivers and streams. Well-constructed watercraft were central to their lives.

Bark-Covered Canoes

The Algonquian and Iroquoian **tribes** of the Northeast cultural area traveled on rivers or lakes in canoes. The Indians made these by stretching large pieces of bark over a frame made of saplings. They used strips of fiber from plant roots to sew each section of bark together. They then sealed the seams with pine pitch to make the vessel waterproof.

The Algonquian tribes were known for their beautiful and lightweight birchbark canoes. A canoe needed to be light because it often had to be carried a short distance between one river or lake and another.

▲ Canoes covered in bark were the most common type of water transportation among the Indians of eastern North America. Their long, sleek design made them easy to paddle. In smaller canoes, paddlers knelt; in larger canoes, which were used to transport goods from place to place, paddlers sat.

MAN'S BEST FRIEND

The dog was an invaluable transportation aid for Northeastern and Southeastern Indians alike. A dog could carry packs or pull a specially designed sled called a **travois** *(truh VOY)*. A travois was essentially a frame of woven saplings. A range of other goods could be strapped to the travois and dragged from one place to another.

The Iroquois covered the frame of their canoes with elm or spruce bark. The bark from these trees is thicker than birchbark. Therefore, Iroquois canoes were much heavier than those used by the Algonquian tribes. Although the added weight was a disadvantage whenever the canoes had to be carried, the thicker bark was an advantage when the canoe was used as a shield against enemy arrows. The Iroquois also used their long and sturdy canoes as ladders to scale walls surrounding their enemies' villages.

Dugout Canoes

Yellow pine and cypress were common trees in the Southeast cultural area. Indians who lived in this area found that the best way to make canoes from these trees was to dig out a cavity in the center of a cut log. Sometimes a boatbuilder first burned the area to be hollowed out to make it easier to work. He might also use water and hot stones to soften the wood. He then dug out the wood using hand tools. A canoe made in this fashion is called a dugout.

The Cherokee, Creek, Seminole, and other tribes of the Southeast all used dugouts to travel the many waterways in their territories. A dugout could be quite swift and sleek. Some of the Seminole dugouts had walls that were only around 1 inch (25 millimeters) thick.

▲ Indians make a dugout canoe in a drawing based upon a 1590 sketch by John White, who visited North America from England. The Indians use fire and hand tools to "dig out" the log that will form the shell of the canoe.

THE FOREST'S BOUNTY

Eastern Indian women were accomplished farmers. However, the men added to the group's diet by hunting and fishing, and the women, by gathering edible plants.

Hunting for Game

Indians of the Northeast and the Southeast most often hunted deer, turkeys, rabbits, and black bears. However, such animals as raccoons, opossums, quails, and pheasants were also a source of meat. The Seminole, who lived in present-day Florida, also hunted alligators and turtles.

Indians used a variety of methods to ensure a successful hunt. A bow and arrow was usually the best weapon for bringing down such larger game as deer and bear. Hunting required a great deal of patience. A hunter often had to spend hours tracking an animal or waiting in hiding before getting close enough to let off a good shot. One method a hunter used to catch deer was to cover his body with the skin of a deer (including its head and horns) and to move slowly toward his prey.

Hunters used blowguns made of river cane to catch such smaller game as ducks and squirrels. The blowguns could be up to 7 feet (2 meters) in length. Young boys learned early how to use a blowgun by shooting at small birds.

Forest Fruits

A variety of edible plants grew in and around the woodlands. Apples, wild berries, mushrooms,

◀ A Powhatan Indian covered with the skin and head of a deer demonstrates traditional hunting techniques. Disguised in this way, hunters could get close enough to deer, which are easily startled, to get off a good shot with a bow and arrow.

FOREST WATERWAYS

The Choctaw, who lived in what is now the state of Mississippi, fished in groups. Men and boys gathered in the shallow waters of a river. They used a trap made of hide that had a drawstring over a long tube of hoops. The trap was large enough that its movement muddied the water. As a result, the hunters could easily spot the fish thrashing around. The men and boys then used bows and arrows to shoot the fish.

walnuts, pecans, and acorns were among the Eastern Indians' favorite foods. Many plants had leaves and shoots that could be cooked and eaten or brewed in hot water to make beverages. In the warmest areas of the Southeast, the range of foods found in the forest was even wider. The Creek and Seminole commonly ate such fruits as wild cherries and grapes, mulberries, persimmons, and plums.

Every spring, the **tribes** living in the northernmost woodlands set up special camps deep in the forests to harvest an especially valued food—sugar. To tap a maple tree, that is, to extract its sweet sap, an Indian carefully made a cut in the tree's bark and inserted a wooden tube. The tree's sap ran down the tube and dripped into birchbark buckets or bowls. When the Indians had collected enough, they boiled it to turn it into maple syrup. If the syrup was boiled even longer, it became maple sugar, which they ate as a delicacy and also used to flavor meat, vegetables, and a range of other foods.

▲ An Ojibwa woman taps a maple tree in a 1908 photograph. The tapping season began in mid- to late winter and lasted from four to six weeks. A maple tree has to grow to at least 10 inches (25 centimeters) in diameter before it can be tapped. It can take 40 years for a maple tree to grow that large.

WORKING THE SOIL

Most of the food the Indians of eastern North America ate they grew themselves. During the lengthening days of late spring and summer, an Indian woman spent many daylight hours tending the rows of plants. Her family's survival depended on her gardening.

The Three Sisters

The Cherokee and Iroquois grew pumpkins, sunflowers, and gourds, but their main crops were beans, squash, and corn. They called these important plants "the three sisters." The Indians chose this name partly because of how they grew the three crops: they always planted beans, squash, and corn together in a single plot as though the three were members of one family.

▼ In a "three sisters" bed, the corn provides a sturdy support for the bean stalks. Squash plants are in blossom at the base of the corn stalks. By planting corn, beans, and squash together, Eastern Indian farmers were able to grow a large quantity of food in a small area.

CORN

Corn was the most important crop to all of the farming peoples of eastern North America. Indians commonly stored corn for use over the winter. They had a number of ways of preparing corn when it was fresh. They roasted it when it was fresh off the stalk. They also boiled it, ground it, and made it into a mush, dumplings, or a pudding. They baked ground dried corn (cornmeal) into bread. Many of the traditional ways of preparing corn continue in modern kitchens, especially in the southern United States.

To grow the three sisters, an Indian woman first made small hills of soil about 3 feet (1 meter) apart using a hoe made of stone or bone. She then sowed several corn seeds into each hill. When the corn started to grow, she added squash and bean seeds to the hills of soil. The beans would grow up the corn stalks, and the squash would spread out between the hills.

The three plants worked together in a unique way. As the corn grew tall, its stalks provided support for the climbing bean plants. The bean plants added to the soil nutrients that fed the corn and squash. The large squash leaves helped to prevent many weeds from establishing themselves in the plot and also gave shade to the shallow roots of the corn. By following this farming tradition, Indians took advantage of the three sisters' different characteristics to maximize the harvest.

Rich Southern Soil

In the warmest areas of the Southeast, where the soil was particularly **fertile**, Indians grew a great variety of crops. The Choctaw were among the region's best farmers. In addition to the three sisters, Choctaw women grew peas, sweet potatoes, melons, and fruit trees.

The Indians of the Southeast, like those of the Northeast, gathered wild fruits and nuts from the surrounding forests. Wild cherries, pecans, chestnuts, and plums grew in abundance. Indians could eat them or dry them and store them for the winter. Nuts and acorns were particularly useful, as they could be stored for many months and also ground into flour.

▲ The Mashpee Indians of Massachusetts used sturdy baskets made of hickory splints during harvest time. The shape of the basket made it easier to spread the weight evenly by placing larger items at the bottom and smaller items at the top. The long straps, also made of wood splints, allowed a person to carry the basket across his or her back.

LEARNING TRADITIONS

▲ A Powhatan woman folds ground corn paste into soaked husks to make corn cakes. Using corn for food and other purposes was a traditional skill passed from mother to daughter.

Indian children in the Northeast and the Southeast learned about all aspects of life from their parents and from other elders of the **tribe.** In this way, knowledge and traditions passed from one generation to the next.

Learning from Stories

All tribes had stories. Some stories taught young listeners the difference between right and wrong. Indians told stories to entertain themselves but also to keep tribal traditions alive. Many stories described important events in the history of the tribe. Others explained a tribe's religious beliefs and traditional practices.

Storytelling might involve elements of performance, with several adults acting out parts in the drama. An actor wore special clothing and a mask and spoke in the character's voice.

Growing Up

Young girls learned the tasks they would need to carry out when they reached womanhood from their mothers and aunts or other female elders. Since farming was the responsibility of women, a girl learned early how to sow and tend crops, where to find wild berries and other plants, and how to prepare farmed and gathered foods. She learned the correct way to cook food and how to smoke meat and fish to preserve them for the winter. Female relatives taught girls how to soften hides and how to make the softened hides into clothing and **moccasins.** As part of this process, a mother would pass on to her daughters her unique beading or **quillwork** designs.

Boys learned from their fathers and sometimes from their mothers' brothers. Boys also needed to learn the tasks they would be expected to perform as men. Boys accompanied older men of the tribe on hunting and fishing trips. They learned how to make weapons and how to defend the village against enemies. Although women grew the food, men cleared the fields. Therefore, a boy learned how to cut down trees and pull out large roots.

THE BEAVER'S TEETH

One Iroquois story offered an explanation of why young children lose their baby teeth. In the story, a mother and father decide that they would prefer their child to have large and powerful teeth like a beaver's. The parents persuade a beaver to trade its teeth for the Indian child's baby teeth. Before long, the beaver realizes that he has not made such a good bargain. He will have a hard time cutting down trees with an Indian child's small and weak teeth. The beaver changes his mind and no longer agrees to the trade. The Indian parents continue to throw their child's baby teeth far into the forest in the hope that the beaver will once again agree to the trade, but the beaver never does. Eventually, when the child has grown a full set of adult teeth, the parents realize that all is for the best. Each creature is given the best teeth for its particular needs.

▲ A Seminole boy using a bow and arrow takes careful aim. Hunting was vital to survival, so it was essential that young Indians acquire the necessary skills.

SPORTS AND GAMES

Indian children were involved from a very young age in the day-to-day responsibilities of village life. Therefore, they spent much of the day doing chores. However, Indians did have some time for recreation. Running, wrestling, and playing ball games were popular among the Indians of eastern North America. They played some games purely for fun. Other games were an opportunity to learn and practice an important skill. A few games formed part of a ceremony.

Games of Chance

Indians of both the Northeast and the Southeast played games of chance that were similar to modern dice games. The Iroquois played the peach stone game during a midwinter ceremony. Six peach stones that had been blackened on one side were placed in a flat-bottomed wooden bowl. In turn, players hit the bowl against the floor so that the peach stones bounced up and fell back down. The number of stones that had landed with the

LACROSSE

Lacrosse was one of the most popular games among eastern Indians. Players used sticks to shoot a stuffed deerskin ball through the opposing team's goalposts and to prevent the opposing team from doing the same. A game of lacrosse could include hundreds of players and could last for several days. To play this game well, an Indian required great strength and endurance—skills that were also important when hunting and fighting. In some areas, players used two short sticks, one in each hand, and would hold the ball with the sticks. In other areas, players used a single longer stick with a pocket at the top for carrying and throwing the ball. A modern version of the game remains popular at high schools and colleges on **reservations** (below) and elsewhere.

▶ Modern Onondaga boys learn how to throw snow snakes. The boys are having fun, but they are also carrying on the tradition of their ancestors—including the rule that girls are not allowed to attend the games. The game of snow snakes involves launching a polished wooden pole along a slick track of snow.

blackened side upward were counted. The player with the highest number was the winner. Choctaw, Cherokee and Creek played the same game but used blackened seeds, corn kernels, or beans instead of peach pits.

Winter Sport

Among the Iroquois, a game called snow snake was especially popular during the winter months. The snow snake was a polished wooden pole from 8 to 10 feet (2 to 3 meters) long with a weighted tip at one end. Indians would create a track by towing a log through the snow. Players then launched their snow snakes down the track. On a slick track, a snow snake could travel as fast as 100 miles (160 kilometers) per hour. The player whose snow snake traveled the farthest along the track was the winner.

Games of Skill

A game involving a hoop and a spear was also popular among Indian children and adults. One player rolled a wooden hoop along the ground, and the other tried to throw a spear through the rolling hoop. In the Southeast, the Creek and Choctaw played a similar game called chunkey. Instead of a hoop, a player would try to hit a smooth stone rolling along the ground. These games were fun, but also helped young players develop the hand-eye coordination necessary for hunting.

MUSIC AND DANCE

Music and dance were a common feature of life for the Indians of eastern North America. Music and dancing were also an important part of religious ceremonies and celebrations. They gave people a chance to express emotions in sound and movement.

Musical Instruments

For many Eastern Indians, flutes and drums were the most important musical instruments. Indians used flutes and drums in a number of ceremonies. Music could be played by drummers alone, by flute players alone, or by a group of musicians playing both instruments. Other music consisted of rhythmic drumming accompanied by singing. Sometimes a man played a flute to attract the attention of a woman.

Iroquois flutes were usually made of such woods as sumac, cedar, and river cane. A wooden flute often had carvings of animal figures or had an

STEALING PARTNERS

In the Southeast, the Choctaw held songwriting competitions between tribes from different villages. The songs could be about animals or people. One Choctaw dance song is called the Stealing Partners Dance. During a performance of this song, the dancers would act as though they were stealing partners from one another. A dancer might also "steal" a partner from a person watching the dance. The tribe that gave the best performance of the song and dance won the competition.

▼ A rattle made of folded hickory bark secured with strips of deer hide. Rattles were an essential part of Eastern Indian dances and might also be made from bones and shells.

end cap in the shape of an animal. The Iroquois and Cherokee also used a water drum. They made this kind of drum by pouring water into a hollowed-out log. They then stretched an animal hide, such as deerskin, across the top of the log and tied it in place. When a musician struck the stretched skin, a distinctive booming sound was produced.

▲ An Iroquois musician beats a water drum with a carved wooden drumstick.

Special Songs

Eastern Indian **tribes** had particular songs to accompany particular activities. Not all songs had words; some consisted of a series of sounds made by the voice. There were healing songs to soothe a sick person into recovery, songs to welcome a newborn baby, and songs to bid farewell to a loved one who had died. Many stories were also sung.

Dances

The Indians of eastern North America also had dances that were unique to each tribe or **culture** group. In the Southeast, the Cherokee, Seminole, and Creek performed the stomp dance during their most important festival, the Green Corn Ceremony. To their lower legs, dancers strapped bundles of turtle shells drilled with small holes. As each dancer brought his or her foot down hard on the ground, the shells rattled together. The air passing through the drilled holes produced a distinctive sound. The clattering shells created a rhythm under the singing that accompanied the dance.

A Changing Way of Life

In the 1500's, European explorers, and later traders and settlers, began to advance into North America. Most European arrivals landed on the East Coast. Therefore, the Eastern Indians were among the first Indian peoples to have extended contact with Europeans.

First Contacts

The first people known to have made contact with the Indians in North America were Norse explorers, who landed on the coast of what is now Newfoundland, in eastern Canada, as early as A.D. 1000. Although these Scandinavian explorers, also known as Vikings, established contact with the native people of North America, **archaeologists** have found no evidence that the groups traded with each other.

▲ The landing of De Soto in Florida as depicted in an 1855 engraving. Hernando de Soto was the first European to explore what is now Florida and the southeastern United States. He arrived in 1539 with 10 ships carrying over 600 soldiers and priests. De Soto believed that there were vast stores of gold in Florida. While searching for these nonexistent riches, he and his men battled and killed Indians from many tribes, including the Creek, Cherokee, and Choctaw. The Spaniards also brought European diseases.

In 1513, Spanish explorers first landed on the coast of Florida. Hernando de Soto led an exploration of the Southeast from 1539 to 1542. De Soto and his men brought valuable trade goods but also European diseases to which the Indians had no natural **immunity** and no medicines to combat them. Within only a few years, a great many Indians of the Southeast had died, especially from smallpox. Some smaller **tribes** were completely wiped out. The population of the Sewee (*SEE wee*) of present-day South Carolina, for example, fell from around 800 to around 50 in less than 50 years.

The first French and English explorers arrived on the northeastern coast during the 1500's. Among the earliest arrivals were traders. They were especially interested in the region's abundant furs. Most of the northeastern tribes were cautious but agreed to trade. Before long, traders from France, England, and other European countries followed,

BOOGER MASKS

During a special dance, the Cherokee made fun of the things they feared. This dance helped them to come to terms with challenges at different points in their history. Young male dancers wore masks with strange and exaggerated features, such as a hairy face or a very long nose. They were known as booger masks. A booger was something frightening, such as a ghost. A booger mask might represent an enemy tribe or a dangerous animal. During a booger mask dance, the male dancers acted rowdily and did things that were usually not acceptable to the Cherokee. They might make rude noises and growl while chasing the women of the village. In later years, many booger masks came to represent the Europeans and the diseases they introduced to the Cherokee. Modern Cherokee still perform the booger mask dance, but only as a form of entertainment.

as did settlers who wanted to establish permanent **colonies**.

Tradition and Innovation

The arrival of Europeans forever changed the Indians' way of life. Some new items, such as iron cooking pots and cotton cloth, benefited the Indians. Most Indians were happy to trade their beaver pelts for the Europeans' brightly colored beads.

At first, dealings between Europeans and Indians were generally polite and businesslike. Often, they were friendly. However, as European countries began establishing more colonies, the Indians had to fight hard to hold onto land that they believed they owned.

◀ William Penn makes peace with the Delaware Indians to protect his Pennsylvania colony in an engraving after a painting by the American artist Benjamin West (1738-1820). There is no written copy of the treaty, but a **wampum** belt was given to Penn by the Indians to record the agreement. This treaty was the first of many that gradually pushed the Delaware and other Eastern Indians off their traditional lands.

FORCED TO LEAVE

During the 1700's, French and British settlers spread through much of the Eastern Indians' territory. Different **tribes** responded to European colonization in different ways. Some fought wars against the colonists. Some made treaties with the colonists. Some Indians sided with the French or British in battles against enemy Indians.

Reservations

The idea of confining Indians to **reservations**—areas of land reserved for Indians—dates from the colonial period. (In Canada, they are called reserves.) Soon after the 13 **colonies** declared independence from Great Britain in 1776, the new American government embraced the idea of Indian reservations.

In theory, reservation land belonged to the Indians. Once a reservation had been defined, non-Indians would never be permitted to take the land away. In practice, formal agreements about reservations were often not honored. In many cases, Indians held onto a reservation only until settlers decided they wanted the land.

▲ *Trail of Tears*, a 1942 painting by Robert Lindneux (1871-1970). In the fall and winter of 1838 and 1839, some 15,000 Cherokee were forced to leave their lands in present-day North and South Carolina, Georgia, and Tennessee and move west to present-day Oklahoma. More than 4,000 men, women, and children died of starvation, disease, and exhaustion during the march, which is known as the Trail of Tears.

Trail of Tears

Beginning in 1830, Americans began to drive the Indians of the Southeast off their land. The Creek and Chickasaw were removed from their homelands in the southern and southeastern United States to lands west of the Mississippi including Arkansas, eastern Texas, and what was then called Indian Territory (present-day Oklahoma).

In 1838 and 1839, the Cherokee were uprooted from their **fertile** farmlands in Georgia and forced to move more than 1,000 miles (1,600 kilometers) west to Indian Territory. Some smaller bands of Cherokee escaped to the mountains of present-day North Carolina. Most, however, endured the punishing 116-day journey west. During the journey, around a quarter of the tribe died. The Cherokee came to call this forced march the Trail of Tears.

Seminole in the Everglades

In the 1830's, the U.S. government staked a claim to Seminole land in Florida. The government ordered the Seminole to move to Indian Territory. Throughout the 1830's, Seminole tribes fought and lost three wars against the U.S. Army. The last Seminole War, fought in 1858, ended with the removal from Florida of 165 Seminole Indians.

Despite American efforts, a few Miccosukee (*mihk uh SOO kee*) Seminole managed to hide in the Everglades, a large wetland area in southern Florida. Finally the U.S. government allowed these Indians to remain there. They continue to live in the Everglades and on some of the Florida Keys.

INDIANS IN COLONIAL AMERICA

During the colonial period, some Indians of the Northeast and the Southeast took on a more European way of life. They felt that the best way to survive was to learn to succeed in non-Indian society. Many Indians gained success and fame in colonial America. For example, Joseph Brant (below), a Mohawk chief, served as a general in the British Army during the Revolutionary War (1775-1783). He did this in return for British promises to support the Mohawk against the colonists. Brant also translated parts of the Bible into the Mohawk language.

LIVING TODAY

The Indians of eastern North America have faced various challenges throughout their history. Many **tribes** continue to preserve the best of their traditions while playing a full role in modern American society.

Independent Governments

When the Indians moved to **reservations**, they lost lands that had been theirs for many generations. Legal treaties define a reservation as a separate nation within the United States, giving each reservation the right to govern itself as the Indians who live on it see fit. Many tribal leaders have used this measure of independence to improve opportunities for young Indians and to further the interests of the tribe.

In the 2000's, the Iroquois continue to view and describe themselves as a **confederacy** of six nations. The Iroquois have built an economy on tourism, forestry, and the sale of arts and crafts goods. They have been involved in construction projects throughout New England. The Mohawk, in particular, are legendary for working with steel at great heights in the construction of skyscrapers and bridges.

The Cherokee tribal government is one of the most efficient in the United States. The Cherokee have built schools and businesses that benefit not only the tribe but also non-Indians. The Choctaw are renowned for their achievement in business. Today, the tribe is among the largest employers in the state of Mississippi.

◀ An Onondaga boy takes part in celebrating his tribe's rich heritage. The Onondaga Nation, near Syracuse, New York, holds several traditional festivals each year.

The Gift of Tradition

Modern Americans are increasingly interested in the traditional practices of the Northeastern and Southeastern Indians. Tribes stage festivals called **powwows** and arrange other celebratory events. They stage these events for the benefit of tribespeople and also the general public. Museums and Web sites provide those wishing to learn more with a wealth of information about the history, **culture,** language, and way of life of America's first peoples.

▶ A group of Cherokee dancers in traditional clothing perform at the annual Chehaw National Indian Festival in Albany, Georgia. Events such as these have become highly popular as Indians seek to reconnect with a past nearly lost.

GLOSSARY

alliance A union formed by agreement, joining the interests of people or states.

anthropologist A scientist who studies humanity and human **culture.**

archaeologist A scientist who studies the remains of past human **cultures.**

artifact An object or the remains of an object, such as a tool, made by people in the past.

banish To condemn a person to leave a community; exile.

breechcloth A garment made up of a narrow band of cloth that was passed between the legs and looped over the front and rear of a belt.

clan A group of people who are related through a common ancestor.

colony A territory inhabited by people who leave their own country and settle in another land; the territory is usually distant from the country that governs it.

conch A large spiral sea shell.

confederacy A league or **alliance.**

constitution The fundamental principles according to which a nation, state, or group is governed.

cradleboard A small wooden frame to which an infant is strapped, usually carried on the backs of the women of most North American Indian **tribes.**

culture A society's arts, beliefs, customs, institutions, inventions, language, technology, and values.

extinct Died out completely.

fast To go without food.

fertile Able to easily produce crops (when used about land or soil).

grave goods Items buried with a dead person, often meant to help and aid the dead in the afterlife.

hierarchy The organization of people into higher and lower ranks.

hunter-gatherer A person who hunts, fishes, and picks wild plants for food.

ice age A period in Earth's history when ice sheets cover vast regions of land.

immunity Resistance to disease.

lacrosse A team sport played with a ball and sticks with net pockets.

lineage Descent in a direct line from an ancestor.

longhouse A large, rectangular dwelling.

mammal The class of animals that feed their young on the mother's milk.

mastodon A large **mammal,** now extinct, similar to a mammoth or an elephant.

matrilineal Tracing family relationships and ancestry through the mother's side.

medicine man An American Indian holy man, such as a priest or healer.

Mesoamerica The area that covers what is today Mexico and Central America.

mica A colored or transparent mineral grouping that separates easily into thin layers.

moccasin A soft shoe, often made from the skin of an animal, and usually not having a heel.

mollusk Any one of a large group of animals having no backbone, soft bodies not composed of segments, and usually covered with a hard shell of one or more parts. Snails, clams, oysters, slugs, octopuses, and squids are all mollusks.

noble A person of high standing in his or her **culture.**

nomadic Moving from place to place in search of food.

obsidian A natural glass formed when hot lava flows onto the surface of Earth and cools quickly.

ordeal A severe and often painful trial, used to test a person's truthfulness, innocence, or strength.

patrilineal Tracing family relationships and ancestry through the father's side.

pendant A hanging body ornament.

poncho A cloth with a slit in the middle, worn as a cloak.

poultice A soft mass of material such as leaves or herbs that is applied hot to the body as a medicine.

powwow A festival at which many different **tribes** meet and that features such performers as storytellers, singers, and dancers.

quillwork Items decorated with porcupine quills.

quiver A case to hold arrows.

reservation An area of land set aside and reserved for American Indians.

ritual A solemn or important act or ceremony, often religious in nature.

sachem The chief of a **tribe** or a **confederacy** among some North American Indians.

snipe A game bird common in marshy areas.

syllabary A writing system in which syllables or sounds are represented by symbols.

tan To make animal skin into leather.

travois A device, consisting of two long poles harnessed to a horse or dog and trailing on the ground, used to transport possessions.

tribe A term that can mean a group made up of many **clans** that shared a territory and spoke a common language.

tunic A loose, short piece of clothing that is slipped on over the head and is often belted at the waist.

wampum Beads made of shell that were used for decoration, as trade items, or to communicate messages or record important events.

wattle and daub A building material made of reeds and clay.

whelk A sea snail with a long curved shell.

ADDITIONAL RESOURCES

Books

Encyclopedia of Native American Tribes
by Carl Waldman (Facts on File, 2006)

The Gale Encyclopedia of Native American Tribes,
Vol. I: Northeast, Southeast, Caribbean
edited by Sharon Malinowski and Anna Sheets
(Gale, 1998)

Indians of the Northeast
by Lisa Sita (Gareth Stevens, 1997)

Indians of the Southeast
by Richard E. Mancini (Facts on File, 1992)

The Iroquois
by Sarah De Capua (Benchmark, 2006)

Myths of the Cherokee
by James Mooney (Dover Publications, 1995)

Myths of the World – Native Americans
by Virginia Schomp (Marshall Cavendish, 2008)

The Seminole
by David C. King (Benchmark, 2007)

Wild Rose: Nancy Ward and the Cherokee Nation
by Mary R. Furbee (Morgan Reynolds, 2002)

Web Sites

http://www.canadiangenealogy.net/indians/index.htm

http://www.nchistoricsites.org/town/town.htm

http://www.native-languages.org/home.htm#list

http://www.nysm.nysed.gov/IroquoisVillage

http://www.seminoletribe.com/history/index.shtml

INDEX

Acknowledgments

The Art Archive: 9 (Laurie Platt Winfrey), 19 (Laurie Platt Winfrey), 55 (Parker Gallery, London/Eileen Tweedy); **Alamy:** 4 (Mark Burnett), 39 (M. Timothy O'Keefe), 46 (Malcolm McMillan); **Bridgeman Art Library:** 16 (Ashmolean Museum, University of Oxford, UK), 20 (British Museum, London/Boltin Picture Library), 21 (Ashmolean Museum, Oxford, UK), 32 (British Museum, London/Boltin Picture Library), 40, 47 (Boltin Picture Library), 56 (Woolaroc Museum, Oklahoma/Peter Newark Western Americana); **Corbis:** 5 (Layne Kennedy), 8 (Lee Snider/Photo Images), 10 (Marilyn Angel Wynn/Nativestock Pictures), 12 (Richard A. Cooke), 22 (Marilyn Angel Wynn/Nativestock Pictures), 23 (Bettmann), 25 (Corey Hochachka/Design Pics), 26 (Bettmann), 28 (Bettmann), 31 (The Mariners' Museum), 34 (Marilyn Angel Wynn/Nativestock Pictures), 38 (Marilyn Angel Wynn/Nativestock Pictures), 41 (Earl & Nazima Kowall), 43 (The Mariners' Museum), 44 (Marilyn Angel Wynn/Nativestock Pictures), 48 (Marilyn Angel Wynn/Nativestock Pictures), 52 (Marilyn Angel Wynn/Nativestock Pictures), 57 (Bettmann), 59 (Kevin Fleming); **Library of Congress:** 14–15, 18, 45, 54; **Nativestock:** 17 (Marilyn Angel Wynn), 24 (Marilyn Angel Wynn), 30 (Marilyn Angel Wynn), 33 (Marilyn Angel Wynn), 49 (Marilyn Angel Wynn), 53 (Marilyn Angel Wynn); **Topfoto:** 35 (The Image Works), 36 (World History Archive), 42 (Michael Schwarz), 50 (John Berry/Syracuse Newspapers/The Image Works), 51 (John Berry/Syracuse Newspapers/The Image Works), 58 (Mike Greenlar); **Werner Forman Archive:** 11 (Peabody Museum, Harvard University, Cambridge, MA), 13 (Field Museum of Natural History, Chicago), 27 (Field Museum of Natural History, Chicago), 29 (Private Collection).

Cover image: **Granger Collection**
Back cover image: **Shutterstock** (Joop Snijder, Jr.)